Oxford Progressive
General Editor

Life Witho
and Seven Oth

CW01664406

M

36p

CANCELLED

The *Oxford Progressive English Readers* series provides a wide range of reading for learners of English. It includes classics, the favourite stories of young readers, and also modern fiction. The series has five grades: the *Introductory Grade* at a 1400 word level, *Grade 1* at a 2100 word level, *Grade 2* at a 3100 word level, *Grade 3* at a 3700 word level and *Grade 4* which consists of abridged stories. Structural as well as lexical controls are applied at each level.

Wherever possible the mood and style of the original stories have been retained. Where this requires departure from the grading scheme, glosses and notes are given.

All the books in the series are attractively illustrated. Each book also has a short section containing questions and suggested activities for students.

LV 04351177

Life Without Katy and Seven Other Stories

O. Henry

Hong Kong
OXFORD UNIVERSITY PRESS
Kuala Lumpur Singapore Tokyo

Oxford University Press

Oxford London Glasgow
New York Toronto Melbourne Auckland
Kuala Lumpur Singapore Hong Kong Tokyo
Delhi Bombay Calcutta Madras Karachi
Nairobi Dar es Salaam Cape Town

and associated companies in
Beirut Berlin Ibadan Mexico City Nicosia

© Oxford University Press 1982
First published 1982
Second impression 1983

OXFORD is a trade mark of Oxford University Press

Retold by Rosemary Border
Illustrated by Kathryn Blomfield
Simplified according to the language grading scheme
especially compiled by D.H. Howe

All rights reserved. No part of this publication may be reproduced, stored in a retrieval system, or transmitted, in any form or by any means, electronic, mechanical, photocopying, recording or otherwise, without the prior permission of Oxford University Press

ISBN 0 19 581403 7

Liverpool City Libraries
CENTRAL JUNIOR LIBRARY
Class 428.6
Access
Price £1.30 Copy
LIVERPOOL CITY LIBRARIES
CANCELLED
CANCELLED

Printed by New Kwok Hing Printing Press Co Ltd.
3/F 44 Lee Chung St., Hong Kong
Published by Oxford University Press,
Warwick House, Quarry Bay, Hong Kong

Contents

O. Henry (William S. Porter) was born in North Carolina, USA in 1862. After only a few years at school he tried various types of work: drugstore salesman; bank teller; journalist; fortune seeker.

He spent three years in prison for embezzlement and it was there that he started writing short stories. After his release he went to New York and continued writing, making the city the scene of many of his stories. These have since become famous for their plain, simple characters and their 'surprise' endings.

O. Henry died in 1910.

1
Life Without Katy

A life without surprises

'Eighty-First Street!' shouted the driver of the bus. A crowd of people climbed out. Another crowd climbed in. The bell of the bus rang – Ding-Ding! and the full bus drove away.

John Perkins walked away from the bus stop. He was on his way home from work. He walked slowly towards Frogmore Flats . . . Frogmore Flats, because he lived there. He walked slowly, because there were no surprises in his life. There was nothing to hurry for. John Perkins was a married man, and he lived in a small New York flat. For people like him, life has no surprises.

'I know what will happen next,' thought John. 'Katy will meet me at the door. She will give me a kiss*. Her kiss will taste of face cream and chocolate. Katy's kisses are always like that. I shall take off my coat. Then I shall sit down. There will be hot beef and boiled potatoes for dinner, and fruit from a tin. After dinner, Katy will tell me about the price of soap. She will tell me about old Mrs Grey . . . the whole story of her day.'

John thought about the evening ahead. At half past seven, the Perkinses always put old newspapers over their furniture. This was because of the fat man in the flat above theirs. He always started his exercises at half past seven. The exercises always shook the ceiling and sent dust down on the Perkinses' furniture.

At exactly* eight, the two men in the flat across the hall always started their quarrel. They always shouted and kicked and threw the furniture about. Just after that, the lady with the pink hair and the jewels always went downstairs. She

**kiss*, a touch with the lips, to show love or as a greeting. **exactly*, in a way which is correct and without mistakes.

LIVERPOOL CITY LIBRARIES
CANCELLED

changed the name over her door bell. Then she was ready for business again. At a quarter past eight Mrs Zanowitski's children always started to cry. The Zanowitskis did not beat their children; the children just did not want to go to bed . . .

And every night, at exactly a quarter past eight, John Perkins always put on his hat. This always made Katy ask, 'And where are *you* going, John Perkins?'

The answer, too, was always the same. 'Just down to the club for a game of cards with the boys.'

John always went to the club. He always played cards with the same friends and he always came home at eleven o'clock. Sometimes Katy was already asleep. Sometimes she was awake and ready for their little quarrel . . . Oh, life in the Frogmore Flats did not offer many surprises.

The note on the table

But tonight things were different. John reached his door, but there was no Katy. No kind, sweet-tasting kiss greeted him. The flat was very untidy. There were shoes and clothes in the middle of the floor. Drawers hung open. That was not like Katy. Then John saw Katy's comb on the floor. Between its teeth was a cloud of her soft brown hair. That made John anxious*. Katy always took every hair out of the comb. She kept the hair in a little blue cloth bag. 'To make a hairpiece,' she once explained to John.

Then he saw the note. It lay on the table.

'Dear John,

I have just had a telegram* from my brother Sam. Mother is very ill. I will take the 4:30 train. Sam will meet me at the station. There is cold chicken in the kitchen. I hope it isn't Mother's bad chest again. Please pay for the milk — 60 cents. She was very ill with her

**anxious*, worried. **telegram*, a kind of letter which is sent very quickly along wires.

chest last spring. Don't forget to write about the electric light. Your clean socks are in the top drawer. I will write tomorrow.

Love from Katy.'

'This is terrible,' thought John. 'We've been married for two years now. We've spent every night of those two years together. I can't believe this is happening.'

He read the note again and again. Here was a sudden change in his way of life. It felt strange and uncomfortable.

Katy's house-coat hung on the back of a chair. She always wore it when she was cooking the dinner. It looked strange and empty, without Katy inside it. A little paper bag lay on the table. In it was Katy's chocolate. The newspaper lay open on the floor. It was open at the 'Trains Today' page. The 4:30 from New York was marked in red.

Everything in the flat looked lost and lonely, because Katy was not there. John stood among these things. There was a strange, heavy feeling* in his heart.

John is sorry

He began to tidy the flat. He wasn't very good at it. Katy usually did it for him. When he touched her clothes, a strange feeling went through him. Life without Katy! He hated to think about it. Katy was a part of his life, like the air all around him. Now, suddenly, she was not there. 'Of course, she will only be away for a few days,' he said to himself. But it did not make him any happier. Katy was gone, and he felt cold and lonely.

John took the cold chicken out of the kitchen. He made some coffee. Then he sat down and ate alone. He remembered the hot beef and boiled potatoes. He remembered the fruit from the tin. He found that he missed them very much.

**feeling*, the way one feels; the sad or happy thoughts that go through one.

So Katy's mother was ill and this was able to change John Perkins's whole life. He finished his lonely dinner. Then he looked sadly out of the window. Outside, the city was coming to life. People were having fun. And he was free! He could stay out until morning if he wanted to. No angry, anxious Katy at home. No questions, no quarrelling. He was a free man.

This examination of his feelings was new to John. He

thought and thought. He began to understand his new, unhappy feelings. While Katy was there, he never thought about her . . . Does a man notice the air around him? Now Katy was gone and suddenly John knew something. He loved Katy and he missed her very much.

'I've acted very badly,' he thought. 'I've been very unkind to Katy. I went out to the club every night. Poor girl – I left her all alone, all evening. I never thought about her feelings.

Well, I've learnt my lesson. When Katy gets home, I'll show her! I'll take her out! I'll give her some fun. I'll pay more attention to her. And I'll stop going to the club – from tonight!'

Outside, the city was calling John Perkins. His friends were waiting for him at the club but John Perkins did not care about them. His Katy was not there. He could not leave her alone. And, because she was gone, he missed and wanted her and he did not want to go out.

A surprise

Near John's right hand stood a chair. Katy's blue dress was on the back of the chair. The cloth still held something of the shape of her body. The dress smelt of her face cream. John took it in his hand. He looked at it, and felt it, and held it to his nose. Suddenly his feelings were too strong for him. He began to cry.

The door opened and Katy walked in. John looked at her stupidly.

'I'm glad I'm back,' said Katy. 'Mother isn't really ill after all. Sam was anxious and he sent the telegram. Then she got better again. He told me at the station. So I took the next train back home . . . Oh, I need a cup of coffee!'

Like a big machine, the Frogmore Flats burst into life. The big wheels turned again. John Perkins's ordinary life began once more. He looked at the clock. The time was exactly a quarter past eight. He put on his hat. He walked towards the door.

'And where are *you* going, John Perkins?' asked Katy.

'Just down to the club,' said John. 'For a game of cards with the boys.'

2
Dirty Money

*A ten dollar bill**

'Money talks,' they say. But surely, you say, a little old ten dollar bill can't talk very loudly? Oh, very well. If you feel like that, don't listen to my story. Go and listen to John D's cheque* book shouting. But don't forget the smaller bills. They can say a word or two sometimes.

I am a ten dollar bill of 1901. Perhaps you have seen a bill like me before. On my face, in the centre, is a picture of an American buffalo. At the sides are the faces of Captain Lewis and Captain Clark. On my back is a picture of a tall woman and some corn. If you take me to a bank you can get ten hard, cold silver dollars for me.

Excuse my rough conversation. A dirty ten dollar bill does not meet many clever people. Most really clever, book-loving people are poor, you see. A ten dollar bill does not often come their way. If it does, they have to go out and spend it at once.

I am six years old now. Many different people have owned me. But a little old torn, damp, dirty five dollar bill gave me a surprise one day. I was sitting beside it in a butcher's pocket. It was dark in there, and it smelt bad.

'Move over,' I said. I gave it a hard look. I don't like being in the same pocket with money like that.

'Don't talk to me like that!' said the five dollar bill. 'I know I'm torn and dirty. I can't help it. I've spent a long time inside someone's stocking, in a big store. My word! It was hot in there!'

'A stocking!' I said. 'How strange! Who kept you there?'

'A shop girl,' said the five dollar bill.

**bill*, a note of money. **cheque*, a written order to a bank to pay money.

'What's a shop girl?' I had to ask.

'*You'll* never know! No shop girl ever sees a ten dollar bill like you!'

Just then a two dollar bill spoke. He had George Washington's head on his face. Now he said to the five dollar bill, 'Isn't a store good enough for you, then? You're lucky. I've just spent a day in a factory. The dust gets in George's throat and makes him cough.'

My life in New York

That conversation took place the day after I arrived in New York. I came in a $500 packet of ten dollar bills. We came from Pennsylvania to a bank in New York.

It is true. We ten dollar bills do not meet many shop girls or factory workers. But we move about a lot. I kept moving too. Sometimes I changed hands twenty times a day. I saw every kind of business and I helped my owners to have every kind of fun. Every Saturday night, someone waved me in a bar and ordered some drinks.

That's an interesting thing. No one waves one and two dollar bills in bars. They slip them across the bar, very quietly. Perhaps they are ashamed of them. I enjoyed those Saturday nights. Sometimes a few drops fell on me. I liked the taste.

Once I was tied up in a big, dirty roll of bills in a market trader's* pocket. I was there a long time, and I hated every minute. The trader was saving his money. He wanted to own a big store one day. So he only spent eight cents a day on food. But one day this trader got into difficulty with the police. I think he put his cart in the wrong place. Well, it cost him a ten dollar bill – me!

The policeman changed me in a cigarette shop. Some men were gambling* behind the shop. One of them was the Chief

**trader*, someone who does business, who buys and sells things.
**gambling*, playing games of chance for money.

of Police himself. He won me that night. He spent me on dinner in an expensive restaurant on Broadway the next evening. I was very glad that I was in the nice end of town again.

In my early days, I did not know about "dirty" money. Then one day I went to a gambling man. His name was Old Jack and his gambling made him very rich. He kept me in a bag with a lot of other bills and some gold too.

Dirty money?

One night a twenty dollar bill spoke to me. 'Well, old Buffalo,' he said, 'you're lucky tonight. Old Jack is going to spend a mountain of money tonight. He offered $50,000 to a church. They refused to accept it. They said that Old Jack's money was dirty.'

'What is a church?' I asked.

'Don't you know? Oh, I forgot. You're only a ten, aren't you? Too big to put in the church collection plate. Too small to buy anything at their Saturday markets. A church, old Buffalo, is a place where they sell combs and pencils for twenty dollars each . . . Something to do with God, I think.'

Well, that twenty dollar bill was right. Old Jack spent a lot that night. The news got around. All along Broadway the jungle animals began to follow us. Perhaps Old Jack's money *was* dirty. But everyone still wanted it. First his friends came. Then friends of his friends arrived. A few of his enemies forgot their quarrels. In the end Old Jack was buying drinks for everyone in town.

At last we came to an expensive restaurant. I knew it well. Several of my earlier owners took me there to dinner. The waiters were anxious to bring Old Jack and his friends the best of everything. But Old Jack was quiet and sad. At last he called the manager of the restaurant. He took a twenty dollar bill from his roll of money. 'Mike,' he said to the manager, 'the church has refused this money. They say it is dirty because I gamble. Will *you* refuse it?'

'Of course not,' said Mike. 'All money is the same to me.'

One o'clock came. The waiters got ready to close the outside doors. Inside, Old Jack was still drinking and spending as fast as before.

The woman

Just then a woman slipped into the restaurant. She went up to Old Jack's table. She was poor; I could see that. Her clothes were thin and old. Her eyes were big and anxious in her white face. She stood there without a word. She looked at the roll of money, then she looked away.

Old Jack stood up. He took me in his hand. Then he gave me to the woman with a smile.

'Madam,' he said. 'Here is a ten dollar bill. I am a gambling man, and the church says my money is dirty. But if you will accept it, this bill is yours.'

The woman took me with a shaking hand.

'Sir,' she said, 'I counted thousands of bills like this one when they were fresh and new. You see, I was a clerk in the bank that made them. The manager of the bank helped me to get that job. To keep that job, he made me . . . Sir, you say this bill is dirty now. I tell you, it was dirty before it reached you . . . But I won't say any more. Thank you with all my heart, sir. Thank you.'

Where do you think that woman took me next? To a baker's shop! She left me there, and she went away with some change* and a bag full of bread and cakes. Of course, I didn't see her after that.

But a week later I met a one dollar bill.

'Hullo, E35039669,' I said to him. 'Weren't you in the change in that baker's shop last Saturday night?'

'Yes,' said the dollar bill. 'She spent E1705143 on milk

**change*, money returned as balance of that given in payment.

and beef. She kept me until the rent* man came. It was a poor room with a sick child in it . . . My word, he enjoyed the food. I expect he was hungry, poor little thing. Then she prayed . . . '

'Prayed?' I said. 'I don't hear many prayers, myself.'

'Ten, you're right. And don't be so pleased with yourself. One dollar bills like me hear far more prayers than you do. She said something about "giving to the poor" . . . Oh, forget it. I'm tired of poor people. You're lucky, Ten. Dirty bills like you meet more interesting people.'

'Be quiet,' I said. 'There's no such thing as dirty money. I know that now. The important thing isn't where a bill comes from. Gambling or church, it's all the same. It's how you spend it. This talk of dirty money makes me tired!'

**rent*, the money one pays to live in a house or flat which one does not own.

3
While the Driver Waits

The girl in grey

The sun went down, and the girl in grey arrived. At the same time every day, she came to the same quiet corner of the park. She sat down on the bench. It was still light enough to read; she took a book out of her bag.

I repeat, her dress was grey. It was very simple and it fitted her well. She wore a grey hat; it hid her face. The face under the hat was calm and beautiful. I repeat, she always came to the park at the same time. And someone knew this.

The young man watched and waited. He said a quiet prayer to the great God Luck. And Luck heard him. The girl turned a page, and her book slipped out of her hand. It landed on the ground a yard away from the bench. This was his chance!

The young man picked up the book at once. He gave it to the girl with a look of hope in his eyes. In a pleasant, ordinary voice he said something about the weather. Then he stood and waited for her reply.

The girl took a long, careful look at him. She saw his ordinary, tidy clothes and his ordinary, pleasant face.

'You may sit down if you like,' she said. Her voice was deep and pleasant. 'Really, I'm glad to see someone. The light is too bad for reading. Perhaps we can talk instead.'

The servant of Luck sat down on the bench beside her. 'Do you know,' he began. (So many young men on park benches begin their conversations in this way!) 'You are the most beautiful girl I have ever seen. Those pretty eyes of yours, my sweet –'

'I do not know who *you* are,' said the girl in a cold voice. 'But you must remember that *I* am a lady. I will excuse you. Perhaps you do not meet many ladies. I asked you to sit down. I did *not* invite you to call me your sweet.'

'Oh, please excuse me,' begged the young man. 'It was my mistake. I mean — there are girls in parks, you know, who . . . Well, of course, you don't know, but some girls —'

Poor little rich girl

'Please, say no more about it. Of course I understand. Now, tell me about those people.' She pointed towards the people who were passing by. 'Where are they going? Why are they hurrying? Are they happy? Tell me about them. Tell me about their hopes and their fears.'

The young man did not really understand. 'Where is this conversation leading?' he thought. But he was anxious to please the girl in grey.

'It *is* interesting to watch them,' he began. 'Really, life is a wonderful thing. Some are going to supper. Some are going to — er — other places. And every one of them has a story.'

'I know,' said the girl in grey. 'I come and sit here because here — here — I can watch ordinary people. Here, I am near the great beating heart of life. In *my* position in life, I can never hear that heart or feel its beats . . . Can you guess why I spoke to you, Mr —'

'Parkenstacker,' said the young man. 'May I know your name?'

'No,' said the girl in grey. She held up a pretty finger and gave a sad little smile. 'My name is too famous. It is very difficult to keep my name — or my picture — out of the newspapers. That is why I am wearing my servant's hat . . . The servants do not understand, of course. My driver thinks I am mad* . . . I spoke to you, Mr Stackenpot —'

'Parkenstacker,' said the young man quietly.

' — Mr Parkenstacker, because I wanted a conversation with a nice, ordinary man. I meet many young men. But all

**mad*, not in one's right mind; silly.

fashionable* young men are spoilt by their money and their position. Oh, I am so tired of it all! Money, money, money! The men crowd round me. They are all the same. They are like expensive little dancing dolls. I hate them! And I am tired of dances, and jewels, and travel –'

'I have sometimes thought,' the young man began, 'that money must be quite a good thing –'

'*Enough* money, yes. But when you have so many millions –' The girl in grey waved her pretty hand. 'It is always the same,' she went on. 'Drives and dinners and dances. Always too much of everything. Rich food and French champagne*. Sometimes the sound of the ice in my champagne glass almost drives me mad!'

Fashionable people

Mr Parkenstacker looked interested. 'I enjoy reading about fashionable people,' he said. 'They interest me. Their way of life is so different from my own. And I have read that fashionable people always cool their champagne in the bottle. They do not put ice in the champagne glass.'

The girl gave a laugh like little silver bells.

'People in my position,' she said, 'love to be different. Just now, it is fashionable to put ice in our champagne. It all started when a king from Tartary visited New York. He had dinner at the Waldorf*, and he put ice in his champagne. Just now, it is fashionable. Soon, everyone will forget about it. Something else will become fashionable instead.'

'I see,' said the young man. 'Of course, ordinary people never hear about these things.'

'Sometimes,' said the girl with a little smile, 'I think about love. I have never given my heart to anyone. But I sometimes think that I could love an ordinary man. A worker, not a

**fashionable*, to do with or done by people who are richer or more famous than ordinary people. **champagne*, a drink made in France in the Champagne region; it is a very expensive drink. **Waldorf*, a famous New York hotel.

passenger on this great ship of life . . . But I expect I shall have to marry someone in my own position. You see, I am a prisoner. A prisoner of my money and position. Just now, two men are begging me to marry them. One is a king's son from a small country in Europe. I think he had a wife, once. He drove her mad, I believe . . . The other is an English lord*. He wants my money, of course . . . Why am I telling you all this, Mr Packenstacker?'

'Parkenstacker,' said the young man. 'I am so glad you decided to tell me.'

The girl gave him a cool, calm look. After all, the differences between them were very great.

A useful job

'What is your job, Mr Parkenstacker?' she asked.

'A very poor one. But I hope that I shall rise in the world. Just now, you said, "I could love an ordinary man". Were you serious about that?'

'Oh, yes. I was serious. But I said "could". I did not say "will". I have to remember the king's son and the English lord, you know. But yes; with the right man, the job is not important.'

'I work,' said Mr Parkenstacker, 'in a restaurant.'

The girl moved a little farther along the bench. 'Not – a waiter?' she said. She looked anxious. 'All work is good and useful, of course. But a waiter –'

'I am not a waiter. I am a clerk.' On the opposite side of the park the word RESTAURANT shone in bright electric letters. The young man pointed towards it. 'I am a clerk there.'

The girl looked at a small gold watch. She rose quickly. She pushed her book into an expensive bag. The book was too large; the bag would not close. 'Why aren't you at work?' she asked him.

**lord*, a man from an important family with a title.

RESTAURA

'I have to work this evening,' the young man said. 'I start in an hour. Can I hope to see you again?'

'I do not know. Perhaps; perhaps not. I must go quickly now. There is dinner, and then a boring party . . . with the same silly people. Fashionable parties are all the same. Perhaps you noticed a large white car at the corner of the park?'

'With a red roof?' asked the young man.

'Yes. I always come in that. Pierre waits for me in the car. He thinks I am shopping in the big store across the road . . . Oh, isn't it silly? I have to lie to my own driver! Good night.'

'But it is getting dark now,' said the young man. 'And the park is full of rough men. Let me walk to the car with you —'

The young man follows

'You want to please me, don't you?' said the girl with a serious look.

'Yes, of course. Why?'

'Then you will stay on this bench for ten minutes after I leave. I do not want to hurt your feelings. I am sure you are honest. But the cars of fashionable people usually carry monograms* . . . Again, good night.'

The girl hurried away. The young man watched her. She reached the edge of the park. She turned towards the corner. The car was still there. The young man now began to follow the girl in grey. He moved in and out of the bushes. She could not see him, but he could see her very well.

She reached the corner. She turned her head and looked at the car but she did not get into it. She passed it, and walked across the street. She walked along the street opposite the park. Then she entered the restaurant with the bright electric name. It was a cheap, shining place with a lot of white paint and glass. The girl went through the restaurant, to a room at the back. There she took off her hat.

**monograms*, the first letters of one's name, made into a pretty design for one's car, writing paper, etc.

The young man saw everything. The clerk's desk was near the door of the restaurant. A girl with red hair came out from behind the desk. She looked hard at the clock. Then she said something to the girl in grey. And the girl in grey took her place at the desk.

The young man put his hands into his pockets. He walked slowly along the street. Suddenly his foot touched something. He looked down, and saw a small book. He picked it up. He saw its bright paper cover, and he knew it at once. '*She* dropped it,' he said. He looked towards the restaurant. Then he thought for a minute. He dropped the book on the ground again, and walked towards the white car.

He climbed into the passenger's seat. He spoke to the driver.

'Take me to my club, Henri,' he ordered.

4
'Girl'

*A visit from a detective**

Room number 962 had a glass door. On the glass in gold letters were the words 'Robbins and Hartley. Traders'. It was half past five. The clerks were all on their way home. The cleaning-women were at work all over the tall office building. Hot city air blew in through the half-open windows of Room 962.

Mr Robbins was fat and fifty. He was still fond of city life. He was getting ready for another evening of dinner and dancing. Mr Hartley lived several miles out of town.

'It's going to be a hot night,' said Robbins. 'You're lucky, Hartley. You can sit out in your lovely cool garden with a long cool drink. *I* have to stay here in all this heat.' Robbins did not really mean it, and Hartley knew it.

He was twenty-nine, with a thin, serious face. 'It's usually cool in Flowerhill,' he said to Robbins. He added, 'But it's usually coolest in winter.'

A man came to the door. He went up to Hartley in a mysterious way and spoke into the young man's ear.

'I've found where she lives,' he said. His voice and his clothes shouted "Detective". Hartley gave him an angry look. He did not want Robbins to know. But Robbins did not notice anything. He was putting his hat on.

'Goodbye, Hartley,' said Robbins. 'Have a nice evening.' He went out. At once the detective became quite ordinary again.

'Here is the address,' he said. He tore a page out of his note-book. Hartley saw, in pencil, the words 'Vivienne Arlington. 341 East – th Street.'

'She moved there a week ago,' said the detective. 'Do you

**detective*, someone whose job is to find out about people.

want me to follow her, Mr Hartley? I can do that for you. Only seven dollars a day, and you'll get a daily report.'

'No, no,' said the trader, 'It isn't anything like that. I only wanted the address. How much money do you want?'

'One day's work,' said the detective. 'Ten dollars will be enough.'

Hartley paid the detective and sent him away. Then he left the office.

Mr Hartley finds Vivienne

One tram took him part of the way. A second tram took him to the poor end of the city. At last he found the street he wanted. The houses were large and old. Once they were the homes of fashionable people. Now they looked ready to fall down.

Hartley found Number 341. It was divided into several flats. On the cheap metal plate above the door was the name 'VALLOMBROSA'. Fire-escapes grew up the sides of the house like strange metal plants. These fire-escapes were full of drying clothes and pale, unhappy children.

Hartley looked down the line of door-bells. He saw the button with 'Arlington' under it. He pushed the button. The front door opened. Hartley went in and began to climb the stairs.

On the fourth floor he saw Vivienne. She was standing by an open door. She invited him inside with a warm smile. She placed a chair for him near the window. Then she sat down too.

Hartley looked round the poor, cheap flat. Then he took a quick, careful look at the girl herself. At last he spoke. 'Good evening, Vivienne,' he said. He thought, 'I was right to choose this girl. She is exactly right in every way.'

Vivienne was about 21. Her hair was red-gold. Every hair shone with its own gentle light. She had pale, clear skin and deep, calm, sea-blue eyes. In her dark skirt and white blouse she looked like a queen.

'Vivienne,' said Hartley with an anxious look in his eyes, 'You did not answer my last letter. I have been looking for you for almost a week. Why have you kept me waiting and hoping like this?'

Will she accept?

The girl looked out of the window. 'Mr Hartley,' she said, 'I do not know how to answer you. You have made me a wonderful offer. Sometimes I feel sure I could be happy with you but sometimes I am not so sure. I am a city girl, Mr Hartley. I have never lived out of town before.'

'My dear girl,' said Hartley in a warm, kind voice. 'I have already told you: I will do anything to please you. You can still go up to town for shops and shows and parties. You can visit your friends in town as often as you like. You do believe me, don't you?'

'Oh, yes,' she said with a smile. 'I know you are the kindest man in the world. I know I am a very lucky girl. I heard all about you when I was at the Montgomerys'.'

'Ah!' said Hartley. His eyes shone. 'I remember that evening well. Mrs Montgomery was saying nice things about you all evening! And she was right. I shall never forget that supper. Come, Vivienne. Promise* you'll come. I want you. You won't be sorry. No one else will give you such a pleasant home.'

The girl looked sadly down at her hands. A sudden terrible thought came to Hartley. 'Tell me, Vivienne,' he asked. 'Is there another? Is there — someone else?'

Her lovely face and neck went very pink. 'You must not ask that, Mr Hartley,' she said in a low voice. 'But I will tell you. There is one other but I have not promised him anything.'

'What is his name?' asked Hartley in a serious voice.

'Townsend.'

**promise*, to agree to do something.

'Rafford Townsend!' cried Hartley. His mouth grew tight and hard. 'How did that man come to know you? And after all I've done for him! He can't, he mustn't do this to me!'

Vivienne was looking down at the street below. 'His car has just stopped outside,' she said. 'He is coming for his answer. Oh, I don't know what to do!'

The door bell rang downstairs. Vivienne pushed the button that opened the door. They heard footsteps on the stairs.

The other woman

'Stay here,' ordered Hartley. 'I will meet him in the hall.' Rafford Townsend came up the stairs three at a time. He looked like a Spanish lord with his light suit and his sharp little black beard. When he saw Hartley, he stopped, and looked rather silly.

'Go back!' said Hartley.

'Hullo,' said Townsend. 'What are you doing here?'

'Go back,' repeated Hartley. 'She's mine.'

'I just came to see a man about some bathroom pipes,' lied Rafford Townsend bravely.

'He's out,' said Hartley. 'Go back.'

Townsend gave Hartley a black look. Then he went downstairs. Hartley went back to his girl.

'Vivienne,' he said, 'I must have you. I will not take "no" for an answer.'

'When do you want me?' she asked.

'Now. As soon as you can get ready.'

She stood before him. She looked straight into his eyes.

'Never,' she said calmly. 'Not while Héloise is there!'

That hurt Hartley. He walked backwards and forwards once or twice across the thin carpet. 'You are right,' he said at last. 'Héloise must go. I refuse to let that woman make me unhappy. You are right, Vivienne. I must send Héloise away before I can take you home. I have decided. I *will* send her away.'

'When will you do this?' asked the girl.

Hartley shut his teeth tight. 'Tonight,' he said. 'I will send her away tonight.'

'Then,' said Vivienne, 'my answer is "yes". Come for me when you are ready for me.'

She looked into his eyes with a sweet, honest look. Hartley could not believe it. She was his at last, and he was the luckiest man in the world.

The dark lady

'Do you promise?' he said. 'Promise you'll come?'

'I promise,' repeated Vivienne softly.

At the door Hartley turned and looked at her. He was so happy. He could not believe his luck. 'Tomorrow,' he said.

'Tomorrow,' agreed Vivienne.

In an hour and forty minutes Hartley stepped off the train at Flowerhill. Ten minutes' walk brought him to the gate of a pleasant little house. He opened the gate and walked through the pretty garden towards his front door. A beautiful dark lady ran to meet him. She put her arms round his neck and gave him a kiss.

'Mother's here,' she said. 'The car is coming for her in half an hour. She came to dinner, but there *is* no dinner!'

'Poor dear!' said Hartley. 'Well, I have something to tell you. I don't quite know how to say this, but —' He bent down and said something into her ear.

The dark lady gave a sudden, sharp cry. Her mother ran into the hall. The dark lady cried out again. 'Oh, Mama!' she said. 'What do you think? Vivienne is coming! She's going to cook for us. She stayed with the Montgomerys' for a whole year. Mrs Montgomery says she's wonderful.' Her eyes were very bright and excited. 'And now, Billy dear,' she said to Hartley. 'You must go straight down to the kitchen and tell Héloise to go. She has been drinking all day!'

5
Hearts and Crosses

'Why aren't you a king?'

Jim Woods put out his hand for the bottle. He got it. Jim usually got what he wanted . . . But this is not Jim's story. He poured out another drink.

'Why aren't you a king?' said Jim again.

Webb Yeager pushed back his hat. He ran his fingers through his yellow hair. This did not appear to help. He took another drink instead.

'You married a queen,' went on Jim, 'but it hasn't made you a king. Do you know what you are, Webb Yeager?'

'What, Jim?' asked Webb. There was a look of hope in his pale blue eyes.

'You're a consort*. They have them in Europe. Over there, that's what they call a queen's husband. A man marries a girl, and she becomes queen. Is he a king, then? No, never in a million years. He's her consort. He's her husband. And he's the father of their children. Yes, Webb, you're a consort. Now why don't you do something about it?'

Jim emptied his glass.

'Jim,' said Webb in a serious voice, 'you and I have worked together since we were boys. I can't talk about this to anyone except you. You worked on the Nopalito Ranch* when I married Santa McAllister. I was the ranch manager then. But what am I now? – Nothing.'

'When old McAllister was the Cattle* King of West Texas,' said Jim, 'you were a very important man.'

'I was,' agreed Yeager. 'Until he found out about Santa and me. Then he kept me as far away from the ranch-house

consort, the husband or wife of a queen or king, who does not rule and is only important because of the person he (or she) is married to. **ranch*, a big farm where cattle are kept on a large amount of open land. **cattle*, all kinds of cows.

as he could . . . Then the old man died. And they started to call Santa the "Cattle Queen." Well, now I take care of the cattle. That's all. *She* looks after all the business. She takes care of the money. I can't buy or sell any cattle myself. That's Santa's job. She's the queen and I'm Mr Nobody.'

'That's wrong,' repeated Jim Woods. 'Why aren't you king? A lot of people think it's strange, Webb. They say, "Why doesn't Webb give the orders?" Now, I won't say anything against Mrs Yeager. She's the nicest little lady between the Rio Grande and the sea. But a man must be the boss* in his own house.'

The heart and the cross

Yeager's smooth brown face grew sad. 'What did you call me, Jim?' he asked.

'A consort, Webb. A queen's husband.'

Webb Yeager picked up his gun belt. 'I have to ride back to the ranch today,' he said. 'I have to send a bunch of beef cattle down to San Antonio in the morning.'

'I'll ride with you as far as Dry Lake,' said Jim. 'I have to look at some young cows there.' The two cowboys* rode away together. They did not say much. Both were deep in thought.

At Dry Lake their paths divided. They smoked a cigarette together. Until then, neither spoke much. Cowboys in Texas are often like this. They can ride for miles without saying a word. They can put a mile, a meal or a murder between their sentences. No one minds. And now Webb added something to their earlier conversation.

'I'm sure you remember, Jim. There was a time when Santa needed me. Old McAllister wouldn't let us see each other? She always told me she needed me.'

' "I'll fill you full of holes if you come near my ranch!" old McAllister said to me. But Santa always let me know.

**boss*, the head man. **cowboys*, men who look after cattle.

She sent our own sign*. Do you remember, Jim — the heart with the cross inside it?'

'Of course I remember that sign,' said Jim. 'All the cowboys knew it. We saw it on all kinds of things. Santa marked it on bags of flour, and newspapers — why, I once saw that sign on the back of a new cook! McAllister sent him to cook for the cowboys. And Miss Santa put her sign on the back of his shirt!'

'Santa's father,' explained Webb Yeager, 'made her promise not to write to me. That heart and cross sign was Santa's own plan. When she wanted to see me, she put the sign on something. And as soon as I saw it, I rode like the wind. We had our own meeting place behind the ranch-house.'

A visitor for Santa

'We knew all about it,' said Jim. 'But we never said anything. You were our boss, and we were on your side. We all wanted you to win the girl. We knew why you kept that fast horse in the camp. And when we saw the sign, we said, "Old Pinto will eat up miles tonight instead of grass." '

'The last time Santa sent me her sign,' said Webb, 'she was very ill. I saw the sign as soon as I reached the camp. I rode Pinto forty miles that night at full speed. She wasn't at our meeting place. I went to the ranch-house. Old McAllister met me at the door.'

' "I won't kill you this time," he said. "I've just sent a cowboy to get you and bring you here. Santa wants you. Go into that room and see her. And then come out here and see me." '

'Santa was lying in bed. She was very ill but she gave me a smile, and she held my hand. I sat down by her bed. I was covered with mud and dust, but she didn't mind. "I've heard you riding across the grass for hours, Webb," she said. "I knew you were coming. Did you see the sign?" "I saw it as

**sign*, something that shows something.

soon as I reached the camp," I said. "You wrote it on the bag of potatoes." '

' "They're always together," she said softly, "always together in life." "Do you mean potatoes?" I asked. I did not understand. "I mean hearts and crosses," said Santa. "Our sign. It means love and pain. You can't have one without the other." '

'Old Doctor Musgrove was standing near the bed. Soon Santa closed her eyes and went to sleep. The doctor felt her face. The fever was gone. "You're the best medicine for Miss Santa," he said. "But you mustn't stay too long. She mustn't get too excited. Go now. The little lady will be all right when she wakes up." '

'I saw old McAllister outside. "She's asleep," I said. "And now you can fill me with holes if you want to. You needn't hurry; I've left my guns behind." '

'Old Mac laughed. "It's bad business to fill a good ranch boss with holes! Where can I get another one like you? I like you, Yeager – as a ranch boss. I just don't want you to marry my daughter but I can still use you on the Nopalito – if you'll keep away from the ranch-house. Now go upstairs and get some sleep. Then we'll talk about it." '

Jim Woods pulled his hat down over his eyes. He got ready to ride away. Webb's horse danced about; it was impatient and anxious to leave. The two cowboys shook hands.

'Goodbye, Jim,' said Webb Yeager. 'I'm glad we had this talk.'

The two cowboys rode away in opposite directions*. A hundred yards away, Jim stopped his horse at the top of a little hill. 'Hey, Webb!' he shouted. Webb Yeager turned towards the sound. 'Why aren't you king?' shouted Jim again.

A quarrel

At eight o'clock next morning Bud Turner tied up his

*directions, north, south, etc. – ways in which to go, or send something.

horse in front of the Nopalito ranch-house. Bud's job was to drive the bunch of beef cattle to San Antonio. Mrs Yeager was outside the ranch-house. She was watering her plants.

Santa McAllister Yeager was very like 'King' McAllister in many ways. She was brave and strong like her father but she had her mother's pretty face and light, strong body. She looked like a queen.

Webb was giving orders to the cowboys. Bud went up to him. 'Good morning,' said Bud. 'Where do you want those cattle to go — to Barber's, like last time?'

Now the queen always decided things like that. She did all the business and her consort took care of the cattle. In the days of 'King' McAllister, Santa helped her father with the business. When he died, she continued, and did it very well. But before she could reply, her consort spoke.

'You drive that bunch to Zimmerman. I spoke about it to him some time ago.'

'Yes, sir,' said Bud.

'Wait!' called Santa quickly. She looked at her husband. There was surprise in her honest grey eyes. 'What do you mean, Webb?' she asked. 'I never do business with Zimmerman. Barber has bought all our cattle in San Antonio for five years. I'm not going to take the business out of his hands.' She turned to Bud Turner. 'Take those cattle to Barber,' she said.

Bud stood and waited. He gave Webb a questioning look.

'I want those cattle to go to Zimmerman,' said Webb. There was a cold light in his blue eyes.

'Don't be silly,' said Santa impatiently. 'Start at once, Bud. Tell Barber we'll have some more cattle for him in about a month.'

Bud looked at Webb again. He looked sorry and uncomfortable. Webb spoke again. 'You take those cattle to —'

'Barber,' finished Santa sharply. 'Go on, Bud. What are you waiting for?'

'Nothing, Mrs Yeager,' said Bud. But he still waited. He wanted Webb to win.

'You heard your boss!' said Webb. He took off his hat to his wife. There was a bitter smile on his lips.

'Webb,' said Santa, 'you're being very silly.'

'What can you expect?' There was a new, bitter sound in Webb's slow, deep voice. 'Let me tell you something. I was a man before I married a cattle queen. Now I'm nobody. I want to be a man again.'

Santa gave him a sharp look. 'Don't be stupid, Webb,' she said in a calm voice. 'Do I ever come between you and the cattle? You know more about them than I do. But I know the business side of this ranch better than you do. I learned it from Dad.'

'Oh, yes,' said Webb. 'I drive the cattle but you're the queen. All right. I'll tell you something now. I'd rather be the boss of a cow-camp than a consort to a queen. It's your ranch. Now Barber can have your beef.'

Webb rides away

Webb's horse was tied to the fence. He walked into the ranch-house. Soon he came out with his best rope and his roll of blankets. He got ready to ride away. Santa watched him. Her face was pale.

From his horse's back Webb spoke again. His serious, smooth brown face was calm but an angry light burned in his eyes.

'There are some cows near the Hondo water-hole. Tell the boys to move them. I forgot to leave orders about it before.'

Santa looked up into her husband's eyes. 'Are you going to leave me, Webb?' she asked quietly.

'I am going to be a man again,' he answered.

'Good luck,' she said in a cold, bitter voice. She turned and walked straight into the ranch-house.

Webb Yeager rode south-east. No one at the Nopalito heard any news of him for a long time.

The months went by, and still there was no news of Webb Yeager. But one day a cowboy called Bartholomew rode past the Nopalito ranch-house. He stopped for a drink and a talk. And he had news to tell.

'Mrs Yeager,' he said. 'I met a man called Yeager down in Hidalgo. He's the new manager of the Seco Ranch. I think his full name is Webb Yeager. He was a tall, quiet man with yellow hair. Is he a member of your family, madam?'

'A husband,' said Santa quietly. 'The Seco Ranch is lucky. Mr Yeager is a very good cattle boss.'

Nothing serious happens when a queen loses her consort. Life continues and Santa found a new cattle boss called Ramsay. He did his work well and life at the Nopalito continued.

Now the Nopalito was famous for its English cattle. For several years before Webb Yeager left, they tried the new animals. They did very well and now they were famous all over the country. Other ranches wanted them too. And so, one day, four young cowboys rode up to the Nopalito ranch-house with a letter for the queen.

An offer from the Rancho Seco

The letter began:

'Dear Madam,

The owners of the Rancho Seco have asked me to buy 100 of your English cattle. If you agree to sell them, please send the cattle with my men. A cheque will follow at once.

Webster Yeager, Manager of the Rancho Seco.'

Business is business. That night the four young cowboys collected the cattle together in a small field near the ranch-house.

Night fell and the house was quiet and still. Did Santa Yeager throw herself on her bed and cry? Did she hold the cold business letter to her heart and cover it with kisses? Or did she just put the letter in her desk with the other business letters? You will never know. But I will tell you one thing —

At midnight Santa slipped softly out of the ranch-house. She turned her face towards the south-east. She sent three kisses in that direction. Then she hurried to the blacksmith's* hut fifty yards away. The fire shone red. Noises of hammering came form the blacksmith's shop.

Later Santa came out with a kind of metal stick in one hand. In the other hand she carried a metal bucket full of red fire. She hurried to the field where the English cattle were.

She opened the gate and slipped into the field. Most of the cattle were a dark red. But one cow was as white as milk. Santa took the rope from her shoulder. She threw it as well as any cowboy. The rope caught the white cow's head. In a few minutes Santa was able to tie the cow to the fence. It was her prisoner. Then Santa ran to her fire bucket and brought out her iron. It was a strange shape, and white-hot.

No one heard the angry voice of the cow when Santa marked it with her brand*. She finished her work, and let the

**blacksmith*, a man who works with hot metal, making shoes for horses, etc. **brand*, a piece of metal which is heated and used to mark an animal. It shows who the animal belongs to.

cow go. Then she ran back to the ranch-house. She cried, just like an ordinary woman, and not like a queen at all.

In the morning the four cowboys drove the bunch of English cattle towards the Rancho Seco. It was a long, slow journey. The cattle had to eat and rest on the way. But one evening they arrived at the Rancho Seco. It was the sixth day, and night was falling. The ranch boss received the cattle. He counted them carefully.

The voice of the king

The next morning at eight o'clock a man rode up to the Nopalito ranch-house. He jumped down from his horse and ran into the house. His horse hung his tired head; it was almost too weak to stand.

But do not be too sorry for Pinto. Today that horse enjoys an easy, comfortable life at Nopalito. He travelled ninety miles that night. No one will ever forget him.

The cowboy reached the house. 'Webb! Webb!' cried a voice. Two arms caught him round the neck.

'I was wrong,' said Webb Yeager.

'Sssh,' said Santa. 'Did you see the sign?'

'I saw it,' said Webb.

What did he see? I am sure you guessed.

'You can be the queen,' said Webb. 'I'm sorry, dear.'

'Sssh,' said Santa again. 'There's no queen here. Come here.'

She led him into a bedroom. There Webb saw a baby. A red, noisy, beautiful baby boy. 'There's no queen on this ranch now,' repeated Santa. 'Look at the king. His eyes are just like yours, Webb. Look at the king.'

They heard the sound of heavy boots outside. Bud Turner came in. His question was the same as always. The question that started the quarrel a year before.

'Good morning. The beef cattle are ready. Shall I drive them to Barber's or –'

Bud saw Webb. He stopped in surprise.

'Ba – ba – ba – ba!' cried the little king.

Webb said exactly the same words as a year before. 'You heard your boss, Bud,' he said. This time he gave the cowboy a big smile.

And that is all. But later the owner of the Seco Ranch went out to look at his new English cattle from the Nopalito Ranch. He said to his new manager, 'What's the brand of the Nopalito ranch, Wilson?'

'X and Y, sir,' said the cattle boss.

'That's right,' said the owner. 'But look at that white cow there. She's got a different brand. A heart with a cross inside it. What brand is that?'

6
After Twenty Years

*The man in the doorway**

The New York policeman walked slowly up the street. He held himself straight and tall. No one was watching, but he did not mind. He always walked like that. It was almost ten o'clock at night. The streets were almost empty. A cold wind was blowing, and it was starting to rain.

As he walked along, the policeman looked around him. He tried several shop doors; he had to make sure they were locked. With his tall, strong body and his honest face, he looked every inch a police officer.

There was not much for him to do tonight. People in that part of the city went to bed early. Now and then you could see the lights of a cigarette shop or a bar. But most of the buildings were ordinary shops and offices. They closed quite early in the evening.

About half way down one of these dark, quiet streets the policeman suddenly stopped. A man was standing in the doorway of a shop. The policeman walked up to him. The man spoke.

'It's all right, officer,' the man said. 'I'm just waiting for a friend. We arranged the meeting twenty years ago. Perhaps that sounds a little strange to you. Well, I'll explain. Then you'll know that I'm not doing anything wrong. About twenty years ago there was a restaurant here, wasn't there? It was called Big Joe Brady's.'

'That's right,' said the policeman. 'Big Joe's was here until five years ago. Then they pulled it down and built these shops.'

The man in the shop doorway took out a cigarette. He lit it. The light showed a pale, square face with sharp eyes. His

**doorway*, opening into which a door fits; a space for a door.

tie-pin was a large diamond.

'Twenty years ago tonight,' said the pale man, 'I had dinner in Big Joe Brady's. I had it with Jimmy Wells. He was my best friend. He was the nicest man in the world. He and I were born here in New York. We went to school together. We played together. We were just like brothers. That night at Big Joe's, I was eighteen and Jimmy was twenty. I was leaving the next morning. I was going out West to make my fortune*. But nobody could make Jimmy leave New York. He thought New York was the only place on earth. Well, that night we agreed to meet here exactly twenty years later. Same time, same place, after twenty years. "Twenty years," Jimmy said. "That will give us time to make our fortunes." '

'What an interesting story,' said the policeman. 'But isn't it rather a long time between meetings? Haven't you had any news of your friend since you left New York?'

'Well, yes. We wrote to each other for a year or two. Then I lost Jimmy's address. I moved about a lot. I expect he lost touch with me too but I know Jimmy will meet me here tonight — if he's alive. He always was the best and truest friend in the world. He'll never forget. I came a thousand miles to stand in this doorway tonight. And I am sure my old friend will keep his promise too.'

The pale man pulled out a beautiful watch. Small diamonds shone on its gold face. 'Three minutes to ten,' he said. 'It was exactly ten o'clock when we said goodbye here at the restaurant door.'

'Did you make your fortune out West?' asked the policeman.

'Oh, yes. I hope old Jimmy has done well too. But he was always rather slow and patient. I had to move and think fast to make my fortune. It's like that out West.'

The policeman smiled. 'Well,' he said, 'that was an interesting story. But I have to go now. I hope your friend arrives.'

**fortune*, a large amount of money.

CLOSED

The meeting

'Of course he'll arrive,' said the pale man. 'He may be a little late, but I won't mind that. If Jimmy is alive on earth, he'll come sooner or later. Good night, officer.'

'Good night, sir,' said the policeman. He walked away.

A cold thin rain was falling, and the wind was stronger. Only a few people were about in the streets. And they hurried along with their heads down and their coat collars up. Still the man stood in the doorway. He waited for his old friend. While he waited, he smoked his cigarette.

He waited about twenty minutes. Then a tall man hurried across from the opposite side of the street. He wore a long coat with the collar turned up to his ears. He went straight up to the man in the doorway.

'Is that you, Bob?' he asked.

'Is that you, Jimmy Wells?' said the man in the doorway.

'Well, well, well!' said the tall man. He took the pale man's hands in his. 'It's Bob! I'm so glad you've come. Well, well! Twenty years is a long time. The old restaurant's gone, Bob. I'm sorry about that. Now we can't have dinner there. But never mind, Bob. Tell me all about yourself. Did you make your fortune?'

'Oh, yes. The West has been good to me, Jimmy . . . You've changed a lot, old friend. You're three inches taller!'

'Oh, I grew a little after I was twenty.'

'Are you doing well in New York, Jimmy?'

'Quite well. I work for the City. Come on, Bob. We'll go and have a drink. We can have a good talk about old times.'

The two men started off up the street like two brothers. The man from the West was beginning to tell his story. The other was listening with interest.

At the corner there was a chemist's shop. It was bright with electric lights. When they reached the hard white light the two men looked at each other. The man from the West stopped suddenly. He let go of the other man's arm.

'You aren't Jimmy Wells,' he said sharply. 'Twenty years is

a long time. But it still can't change the shape of a man's nose.'

'It sometimes changes a good man into a bad one,' said the tall man. 'You've been under arrest* for ten minutes, "Slippery" Bob. The Chicago police want a word with you. They sent us a telegram about you. Your photograph is in all the police stations in the city. You'll come quietly, won't you? Good. Now, before we go to the police station, here's a note. Officer Wells asked me to give it to you. You can read it here by the window.'

The man from the West took the little piece of paper. In the electric light he read the few short lines. His hand shook.

> 'Bob — I was there at the right time. I saw you in the doorway. When you lit your cigarette, I saw your face. I remembered your photograph in the police station. The Chicago police want you, Bob, and I have my job to do. But I couldn't make the arrest myself. I asked a detective to do it.
>
> JIMMY.'

**arrest*, the act of taking a person prisoner by a policeman.

7
The General and the Gold*

El Refugio

Some stories are just for fun. Other stories try to teach the reader something. That kind of story is often very boring. The story I am about to tell is like that. So we'll have the boring part first.

'Not everything that shines is gold,' they say. Yes. It is wise to test it first.

In one part of New York many Spanish and South American people live. These few streets are like a little sunny corner of the cold city. The centre of life in this part of town is a little restaurant. Its name is El Refugio. All the Spanish and South American people go there. They come from Chile and Colombia and Bolivia. They escape from their mad governments. They come to New York. And in New York they all meet in El Refugio. There they plan revolutions*. They arrange to send guns to South America. They collect money to pay for this. But most of the time they just talk and play cards. They know they are always welcome.

The food at El Refugio is wonderful. Are you tired of the French food in the fashionable restaurants? Then hurry to El Refugio. They will give you wonderful fresh fish. They cook it with oil and wine* in the Spanish way. It tastes – but no! I cannot describe it. You must taste it for yourself. It is the food of the gods.

One day a ship reached New York from Colombia. One of its passengers was General Perrico Ximenes Villablanca Falcon. The General had a brown face. He measured forty two inches around the middle. He was five feet four inches

**General*, an important officer in the army. **revolutions*, the acts of taking over a country and throwing out the old government and rules. **wine*, a drink made from fruit; too much wine will make you drunk.

tall in his expensive Spanish boots. He wore beautiful, expensive clothes and he looked very important.

General Falcon spoke some English. He was able to ask the way to a street in the Spanish part of the city. El Refugio stood in that street, but the General was not looking for a restaurant. He wanted a hotel.

He reached the street without any difficulty. He found a pleasant, clean red brick house. Outside it was a sign.

Mrs O'Brien

'Hotel Espanol', said the sign. And in the window was a card. On it were the words, 'Spanish Spoken Here.' The General went in. 'I am sure they will make me welcome here,' he said to himself.

In the pleasant little office was Mrs O'Brien. She was the manager of the hotel. Her hair shone like gold. She had a pink, pleasant face. She was also very fat. General Falcon took off his hat like a true gentleman. Then he spoke to her in very loud, fast Spanish.

'Oh, you speak Spanish?' said Mrs O'Brien in English.

'I am from Colombia, Madam,' said the General (also in English). 'I speak Spanish. And the card in your window says "Spanish Spoken Here." '

'That's right,' said Mrs O'Brien. 'You've just spoken Spanish, haven't you? But I'm sure *I* can't speak a word of Spanish!'

General Falcon took a room at the Hotel Espanol. The absence of Spanish did not appear important to him now. He made himself comfortable. In the evening he went out into the street. He wanted to see this great city for himself. He thought about Mrs O'Brien and her wonderful hair. 'Here,' he said to himself, 'here are the most beautiful ladies in the world. No Colombian lady is as lovely as the ladies of New York. And Mrs O'Brien is the loveliest of all. But no! General Falcon must not think of love and beauty. He must think only of his country. He has a job to do!'

At the street corner the General had great difficulty with the traffic. A tram almost knocked him down. He moved back to avoid it, and a bus almost ran over him. Then he had to jump out of the way of a taxi. This made him knock against a street trader's cart. Some oranges fell off the cart

and the trader was angry. The General did not understand all the man's words. But he understood his feelings. He tried to escape.

Two criminals saw the General. Both knew at once that he was a stranger. One of the criminals was Big Bill McGuire. He had a strong arm and a piece of heavy iron pipe. The other was Baby Face Kelly. He did not use iron pipes. He was too clever for that.

A new friend

Kelly reached the General first. 'Go away,' he said to Big Bill McGuire. 'He's mine. I saw him first.'

'Excuse me,' said Kelly to the General, 'I see that you are in difficulty. Let me help you.' He picked up the oranges and spoke to the trader. Then he took the General by the arm. The General was glad. He needed a friend in this big, noisy, mad city.

'A thousand thanks, kind sir,' he said to Kelly. 'I am trying to get back to the hotel of Mrs O'Brien. I am staying there. I went out for a little walk. But the traffic goes so fast. And everyone is in such a hurry.'

'You can't go back alone,' said Kelly. 'I'll take you. What's the address?' They went back to the hotel together.

At the door of the Hotel Espanol they stopped. A little further down the street the electric sign of El Refugio shone. Kelly knew New York very well. He knew the little restaurant too.

'Say, General,' he said, 'why don't we go there and have a drink?'

'A very good idea, sir,' said the General.

An hour later the General and Kelly were in a dark corner of the restaurant. Bottles and glasses stood on the table between them. For the tenth time, the General told Kelly his secret*.

**secret*, something which must be kept from other people.

'You ask why I come here, my friend. Well, I will tell you. But it is a secret. I have to buy guns for the revolution in Colombia. I have cheques for twenty-five thousand dollars in my pocket.'

At the other tables were other leaders of other revolutions. They were telling their secrets too, in loud, excited voices. But the General shouted loudest of all. He beat upon the table. He shouted for more wine. 'You understand,' he shouted to his new friend, 'all this is a deep, dark secret. You must not say a word about it to anyone.'

Kelly promised. He became quite excited about it all. He reached across the table and took the General's hand.

'General,' he said, 'I don't know where your country is. But I'm on your side. I'll help with your revolution. You were lucky to find me. I'm the only man in New York who can buy these guns for you. The boss of the War* Office is my best friend. He's in New York now. I'll go and see him tomorrow. Meanwhile, keep those cheques safe. I'll call for you tomorrow. And I'll take you to see him.' Then a thought came to him suddenly. 'I say, you aren't talking about Columbia in the U.S.A., are you? You can't take that with only two thousand guns. Someone once tried it, and failed.'

Kelly makes a call

'Oh, no!' said the General. 'I am talking about Colombia – Colombia, with an O. It is a great country in South America.'

'I'm glad about that,' said Kelly. 'Now I'll take you to your hotel, General. You need some sleep. I'll call the boss of the War Office tonight. I'll arrange the meeting. It will be difficult to get the guns out of New York. I don't know anyone who can do it. Except me, of course.'

They said goodbye at the door of the Hotel Espanol. The General looked up at the moon with large, dark, sad eyes.

'Your New York is a great city,' he said. 'The traffic goes

**war*, fighting.

so fast and makes so much noise. And everyone is in such a great hurry. But ah! Mr Kelly – the ladies! They are so beautiful, with their hair of gold and their big, warm bodies . . . They are wonderful! Really wonderful!'

Kelly said goodbye and went to the nearest telephone box. There he called McCrary's bar on Broadway. He asked for Jimmy Dunn.

'Jimmy Dunn here,' came the answer at last.

'You're not Jimmy Dunn,' said Kelly with a laugh. 'You're the new big boss of the War Office.'

'Who says? You're mad!'

'I say, and I'm not mad . . . It's Kelly here, Jimmy. I've got a wonderful new plan. There's a General from somewhere in South America. We'll both make our fortunes. Wait for me at McCrary's. I'll be with you in ten minutes.'

Jimmy Dunn was a very clever criminal. He was an artist in his own way. He did not need guns or iron pipes. He did not use poison. People liked him and believed in him. He did not need to steal their money. They just put it into his hands. Kelly thought Dunn was wonderful. He wanted to be just like him, one day.

Kelly soon arrived at McCrary's bar. The two men had a long talk. Kelly explained all about the General.

'It'll be easy, Jimmy. He's from Colombia. There's a war, or a revolution, or something, out there. They've sent him here. He has to buy two thousand guns. He showed me some cheques for twenty-five thousand dollars. It's true, Jimmy. Of course, I really wanted thousand-dollar bills. Bills are always easier than cheques. Now we'll have to wait until he goes to the bank.'

Never hurt a lady's feelings

They talked for two hours. At the end Dunn said, 'Bring him to Number – Broadway at four o'clock tomorrow afternoon. I'll have everything ready.'

Kelly called at the Hotel Espanol just before four the next day. He found him in conversation with the lovely Mrs O'Brien.

'I've arranged everything,' he said to the General. 'The boss of the War Office is waiting for us.'

The General said a sad goodbye to Mrs O'Brien. He turned to Kelly. 'Yes, kind sir,' he said. 'My country is more important than my feelings. But the ladies of New York are so beautiful! Look at Mrs O'Brien. Isn't she wonderful? A consort for a god. Her hair is like threads of gold.'

Now Mr Kelly loved to make jokes. He made one now. He was sorry about it later.

'That colour came out of a bottle,' he said. 'You know what they say, General. "Not everything that shines is gold!" '

Mrs O'Brien heard. She lifted her head. For a few seconds she looked hard at Kelly. She watched him leave with the General, and her eyes were full of hate. It is always unwise to hurt a lady's feelings.

Soon the brave General and his new friend arrived at the address in Broadway. A clerk greeted them. 'Wait here, please,' he said. They waited for half an hour. Then the clerk led them into a beautiful big office. A man was sitting at a desk.

The War Office Chief

'General,' said Kelly. 'This is the head of the War Office of the United States Government. He is a very busy man. But he has agreed to see you today . . . Sir, this is General Falcon.' He quickly explained the General's part in the revolution in Colombia.

'Ah – Colombia!' said the great man. 'That will be rather difficult. The head of your government and I do not agree about everything . . .' He gave General Falcon a mysterious little smile. 'You see, I agree with you, General. I want to help you. Now, you know that it is not easy to send guns out of my country. Everything has to pass through the War Office. Now, General, I shall do my best for you. Any friend of Mr Kelly is a friend of mine but you must keep this a secret. I do not want to start a war between your country and mine. Now I will send for my clerk. I do not know how many guns we have just now. He will be able to tell us at once.'

The big boss rang a bell. The clerk came into the room.

'We need two thousand guns in a hurry,' said the boss. 'What have you got?'

The clerk went out for a minute. He returned with a big red book. 'Well, sir, there are two thousand guns *here*,' he said. He opened the red book and pointed with his finger. 'The King of Morocco wanted them. But he forgot to send the money with his order. You know our rules, of course, sir. No money, no guns.'

'That's right,' said the great man. 'You may go.' He turned to the General. 'General Falcon, we can let you have the guns. And now, please excuse me. I am expecting an important Japanese General.'

'How can I ever thank you, Mr Kelly?' said the General.

'Oh, you can buy me a drink,' said Kelly. 'I'm glad I was able to help you.'

Mrs O'Brien's offer

Soon Jimmy Dunn was very busy. He and his friend bought a lot of empty gun boxes. They filled them all with old bricks. Then they put them in an old empty factory.

Meanwhile the General returned to the Hotel Espanol. Mrs O'Brien spoke to him at once.

'Excuse me General, but what are you doing with that no-good Irishman?'

'Madam!' cried the General. 'You must not speak like that about Mr Kelly. He is my good friend.'

'Come into the garden,' said Mrs O'Brien. 'I want to talk to you.'

An hour passed. Then the General spoke. 'And you say I can buy this lovely house for eighteen thousand dollars? This lovely house, and its beautiful garden?'

'That's right,' said the lady. 'And it's cheap at that price.'

'Ah!' said the General. 'Why am I thinking of war and revolution? This place is so lovely. I want to stay here always. Other brave men can continue the war. My place is here. We will buy the Hotel Espanol. And you will be mine for ever!'

Mrs O'Brien rested her head on the General's broad shoulder. Her hair shone brighter than ever.

The end of the story

'You will have the guns in two days,' was the great man's promise to the General. The boxes of bricks were ready.

'Bring him,' Dunn told Kelly. 'Tell him to change his cheques at the bank first.'

Kelly hurried to the Hotel Espanol with his news. He found the General at the desk in the hall.

'I have decided,' the General said. 'I am not going to buy the guns after all. Today I have bought this hotel and all its furniture. I am going to marry the lovely Mrs O'Brien to-morrow.'

Kelly's mouth hung open for a minute. Then his face turned dark red. 'You – you thief!' he shouted. 'You criminal! You've bought the hotel with your country's money!'

'Ah,' said the General. 'War and revolution are not nice, my friend. I am tired of shooting people. I am tired of war and revolution. I shall live here in peace with my lovely lady. Ah! Her hair! It is like threads of gold!'

Kelly was unable to speak.

'Ah, Mr Kelly,' said the General sweetly. 'How can you understand? *You* have never eaten Mrs O'Brien's chicken soup!'

8

*The Love of a Busy Businessman**

The secretary and the businessman

Pitcher was the chief clerk in the office of Harvey Maxwell. Mr Maxwell was a businessman. He bought and sold things. He also arranged for other businessmen to do so. Pitcher was an important man in his office.

This morning Pitcher's usually calm face wore a look of surprise. The clerk did not usually show his feelings but today his boss came into the office late. It was half past nine. And he had his pretty young secretary* with him.

With a quick 'Good morning' Maxwell hurried to his desk. Hundreds of papers waited for him there. He buried himself in them at once.

The secretary was beautiful. She did not look or dress like a secretary. Her simple clothes and hair were most pleasant to see. And this morning her face shone with a gentle light. Her eyes were bright and full of dreams.

Pitcher noticed this. He also noticed a difference in her ways this morning. She usually went straight into her office. Today she stayed near Mr Maxwell's desk. But he did not notice her. As soon as he sat down at the desk, Maxwell became a machine.

At last he saw her. 'Well, what is it?' he asked sharply. His cold grey eyes looked at her impatiently.

'Nothing,' said the secretary. She moved away with a little smile. 'Mr Pitcher,' she said to the clerk. 'Did Mr Maxwell say anything about the agency* yesterday?'

'About getting another secretary, Miss Leslie? Yes, he did. He told me to telephone the agency. I did. I told them to

**businessman*, a man whose job is business, buying and selling and making money. **secretary*, someone (usually a woman) whose job it is to help someone by taking telephone calls, writing letters, etc. **agency*, a business which sends people to jobs and gets jobs for its customers.

send me a secretary this morning. But it's a quarter to ten now, and no one has arrived yet.'

'I will just continue my work, then,' said the secretary. 'Just until the new secretary arrives.' She went into her office. She hung up her hat and started to work.

Perhaps you have never seen a really busy New York businessman at work.

'One crowded hour of busy life,' the old song says. Mr Maxwell's hours were crowded. The minutes and seconds were fighting for a place in them.

The girl from the agency

And this day was Harvey Maxwell's busiest day. The telephone rang all the time. He was buying, selling, arranging. Visitors came and went. The clerks in the office flew about like leaves in a storm. Pitcher's usually calm face was anxious.

Business was fast and fierce. Prices flew up and down and Maxwell had to follow them exactly. He moved among his business machines and telephones. He gave orders . . . he was in another world.

In the middle of all this, the businessman suddenly noticed a stranger. It was a young woman with a lot of bright yellow hair. She wore a large green hat and a white coat with black fur on the collar. Pitcher appeared at her side.

'A young lady from the agency, sir,' he said. 'About the job.'

Maxwell turned round in his big chair. His hands were full of papers. 'What job?' he asked.

'The job of secretary, sir,' said Pitcher. 'You asked me to call the agency yesterday. You wanted them to send you a new secretary this morning.'

'Pitcher, you are going mad,' said the businessman. 'I do not need a new secretary. Miss Leslie has been with me for a year. I am very pleased with her. She is a very good secretary . . . Madam,' he said to the young woman. 'I am sorry. There is no job here.' He turned to Pitcher. 'Tell the agency that you made a mistake. Don't bring any more secretaries in here.'

The young woman left the office. There was an angry look on her face, under the large hat. Oh dear, thought Pitcher. The boss has forgotten!

Business continued. Orders to buy and sell flew about like birds. Maxwell still worked like a machine. He worked quickly and exactly. This was the world of business and money. There was no time for feelings.

Lunch time came. The office was a little calmer now. Maxwell stood by his desk. His hands were full of letters and telegrams. His pen was behind his ear. His hair hung on his face in damp strings.

The scent of flowers

The window of his office was open. Spring was coming to the city. And through the window came a soft, sweet scent* of spring flowers. For a second Maxwell stood still. He knew that scent. His secretary always wore it. The scent brought Miss Leslie into Maxwell's busy thoughts. Suddenly the world of business appeared very unimportant. She was in the next office and he had something to say to her.

'I'll do it now,' Maxwell said to himself. 'Why didn't I do it long ago?'

He burst into his secretary's office. She looked up at him with a smile. Her face was pink and her eyes were honest and kind. Maxwell sat down on the edge of her desk. His hands were still full of papers. His pen was still behind his ear.

'Miss Leslie,' he began. 'I can't stay here long. I am very busy but I want to say something to you. Will you be my wife? I haven't had time to make love to you in the ordinary way but I really do love you. Answer quickly, please. I must get back to work.'

**scent*, pleasant smell.

'Oh, what are you talking about?' cried the secretary. She looked at him with round, anxious eyes.

'Don't you understand?' went on Maxwell. 'I want to marry you. I love you, Miss Leslie. I wanted to tell you. I waited for a quiet time; I was too busy before . . . Oh, dear. There's another telephone call for me now. Tell them to wait a minute, Pitcher . . . Miss Leslie, will you marry me?'

The secretary acted in a very strange way. At first she was too surprised to move or speak. Then she cried. Then she smiled, like sun after rain. One of her arms slipped round the businessman's neck.

'I know now,' she said softly. 'You're so busy, dear. It really makes you forget *everything*, doesn't it? Harvey, have you really forgotten? We were married yesterday!'

Questions

1
Life without Katy

A. John lived in: New York/Los Angeles/a small town in America.
B. Katy: never gave John a kiss/always gave him a kiss when he came home/always gave him a kiss when they said goodnight.
C. The flats: were always very quiet/were noisy in the mornings/were noisy in the evenings.
D. John's wife Katy left him: because she did not love him/ because her mother was ill/because she wanted to see her brother Sam.
E. When Katy came home: John got ready to go out to the club/gave her a big kiss/started to cry.

2
Dirty Money

A. Which bill in the story had a picture of George Washington on?
B. Why did the twenty dollar bill call 'our' bill "Old Buffalo"?
C. In your own words, tell the story of the woman and Old Jack.
D. What did the woman spend the money on?
E. What does the writer mean by "dirty money"?

3
While the Driver Waits

Fill in the 'holes' with the correct words. Here are the words:
heart tired rich grey hid bench famous
The sun went down and the girl in ( ) sat down on the ( ). Her hat ( ) her face. She liked to sit and watch the people. She felt she was near the great beating ( ) of life. She did not tell the young man her name because that name was too ( ). She told him she was ( ) of her life as a ( ) lady.

4
'Girl'

At the beginning of this story, the reader thinks Mr Hartley is looking for a wife, and not for a cook. What happens later in the story which shows he wants a cook, not a wife? How early in the story did *you* guess?

5
Hearts and Crosses

A. Webb Yeager and Jim Wood were: traders/cowboys/blacksmiths.
B. Santa owned a big: ranch/store/factory.
C. Santa marked her sign for Webb because: she could not write/Webb could not read/old McAllister would not let her write to him.
D. As soon as he saw the sign Webb always: wrote Santa a letter/rode to the ranch at once/sent a cowboy to see her.
E. The new 'king' of the ranch was: Webb/the new manager/the baby.

LIVERPOOL CITY LIBRARIES CANCELLED

6
After Twenty Years

A. Who was Big Joe Brady? Do we meet him in the story?
B. What things in the story tell us that the man in the doorway is rich?
C. How did the man in the doorway know that the other man was not his friend Jimmy?
D. Why didn't Jimmy make the arrest himself?
E. Was Jimmy right to do what he did?

7
The General and the Gold

A. 'Not everything that shines is gold', the story says. Is this true? Can you tell a little story to show it?
B. Where exactly is Colombia? And where is Columbia?
C. There are several dishonest people in this story. Who is the worst? Why do you think so?
D. Do you feel sorry for Kelly and Dunn? Explain why you feel as you do.
E. Travel forward five years. How are the General and Mrs O'Brien? Are they happy? What are Kelly and Dunn doing now?

8
The Love of a Busy Businessman

Fill in the 'holes' with the correct words. Here are the words:
businessman secretary agency telephone telegram

A. We send a ( ) when we want to tell someone something in a hurry.
B. The ( ) helped us to find a new office girl.
C. A ( ) call to London from Hong Kong costs a lot of money.
D. The ( ) came into the office and stood beside her boss's desk.
E. Mr Maxwell was a busy ( ).

Oxford Progressive English Readers

Introductory Grade

Vocabulary restricted to 1400 headwords
Illustrated in full colour

The Call of the Wild and Other Stories	Jack London
Emma	Jane Austen
Jungle Book Stories	Rudyard Kipling
Life Without Katy and Seven Other Stories	O. Henry
Little Women	Louisa M. Alcott
The Lost Umbrella of Kim Chu	Eleanor Estes
Stories from Vanity Fair	W.M. Thackeray
Tales from the Arabian Nights	Retold by Rosemary Border
Treasure Island	R.L. Stevenson

Grade 1

Vocabulary restricted to 2100 headwords
Illustrated in full colour

The Adventures of Sherlock Holmes	Sir Arthur Conan Doyle
Alice's Adventures in Wonderland	Lewis Carroll
A Christmas Carol	Charles Dickens
The Dagger and Wings and Other Father Brown Stories	G.K. Chesterton
The Flying Heads and Other Strange Stories	Retold by C. Nancarrow
The Golden Touch and Other Stories	Retold by R. Border
Great Expectations	Charles Dickens
Gulliver's Travels	Jonathan Swift
Hijacked!	J.M. Marks
Jane Eyre	Charlotte Brontë
Lord Jim	Joseph Conrad
Oliver Twist	Charles Dickens
The Stone Junk	Retold by D.H. Howe
Stories of Shakespeare's Plays 1	Retold by N. Kates
Tales from Tolstoy	Retold by R.D. Binfield
The Talking Tree and Other Stories	David McRobbie
The Treasure of the Sierra Madre	B. Traven
True Grit	Charles Portis

Grade 2

Vocabulary restricted to 3100 headwords
Illustrated in colour

The Adventures of Tom Sawyer	Mark Twain
Alice's Adventures Through the Looking Glass	Lewis Carroll
Around the World in Eighty Days	Jules Verne
Border Kidnap	J.M. Marks
David Copperfield	Charles Dickens
Five Tales	Oscar Wilde
Fog and Other Stories	Bill Lowe
Further Adventures of Sherlock Holmes	Sir Arthur Conan Doyle